11/07

DIGITAL CAREER BUILDING™

CAREER BUILDING THROUGH

DIGITAL MOVIEMAKING

MIRIAM SEGALL

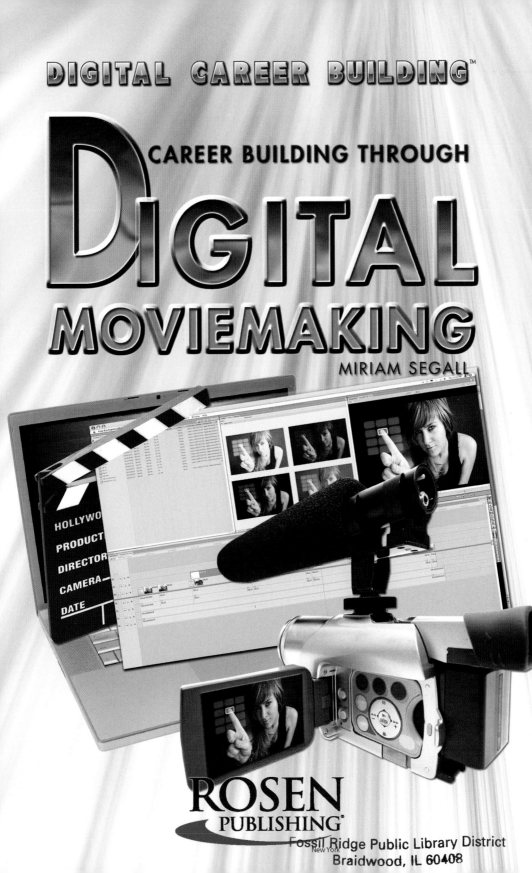

ROSEN
PUBLISHING®

New York

Published in 2008 by The Rosen Publishing Group, Inc.
29 East 21st Street, New York, NY 10010

First Edition

Library of Congress Cataloging-in-Publication Data

Segall, Miriam.
Career building through digital moviemaking / Miriam Segall.
    p. cm. — (Digital career building)
Includes bibliographical references.
ISBN-13: 978-1-4042-1945-8
ISBN-10: 1-4042-1945-5
1. Digital cinematography—Vocational guidance—Juvenile literature.
2. Motion pictures—Production and direction—Juvenile literature. I. Title.
TR860.S38 2008
778.5'3024—dc22

                                                            2007001107

Manufactured in the United States of America

CONTENTS

CHAPTER ONE
AN INTRODUCTION TO DIGITAL MOVIEMAKING

When *Time* magazine declared that YouTube—the Web site that allows anyone to upload and view countless video clips—to be the Best Invention of 2006, it cemented what has become one of the biggest online phenomena in a short period of time. From anywhere in the world, a person can post movie clips, funny videos, and in-progress events for all to see. Some people who have appeared on videos that received many hits on YouTube and became "viral" (shared and forwarded among many computer users) have become celebrities. Others have parlayed their YouTube exposure and popularity into more lucrative jobs and professional opportunities.

In response to the rise of YouTube and other sites that encourage user-generated content, *Time* declared the PC user as 2006 Person of the Year.

But the most important reason that the YouTube site has become, as of this writing, the most popular on the World Wide Web—even more so than the search engine Google and the social networking site MySpace—is because it's easy to use. Seconds after uploading a video, you can make it available on your own Web site with simple code, and thousands of potential viewers can see it, pass it along, and spread the word. No wonder Google spent $1.65 billion to buy YouTube in October 2006—a huge sum of money for what is essentially a repository of mostly amateur or dated videos.

Many YouTube users are young people. The site has been embraced by teenagers who aren't just watching videos; they are also creating and marketing them. Making digital films and videos has never been easier or cheaper. As a result, more are embracing the medium and achieving high-quality results. In their films and videos, teens are speaking out about issues, trying to create high art, or just having fun with their digital video cameras. How did this come about, and how can others get in on the action? These questions, as well as an overview of how teens can use their moviemaking prowess for critical acclaim and financial gain, will be answered over the course of this book.

The History of Digital Moviemaking

Digital moviemaking began to emerge in the 1980s, when early experiments with the format, met with limited success. The technology improved significantly in the mid-1990s with the introduction of the MiniDV format in Sony's DCR-VX1000 camcorder (a handheld digital video

A Sony employee shows off the company's new mini digital camcorder, the DCR-PC1000, in 2005. It features a dynamic range that allows for better lighting detail on both video and still images.

camera). MiniDV offered much greater quality than previous analog formats at the same price point. In other words, you could achieve much better results, while paying the same price for an analog version that would provide you with lower-quality images.

While its quality was superior to that of analog video, these MiniDV camcorders were not considered as good as traditional film. Yet the camcorders, in conjunction with nonlinear editing software that could run on personal computers, allowed many people to begin making movies. They were previously prevented from doing so by the high costs of shooting on film and processing (developing) that film.

It wasn't until May 2002, however, that digital filmmaking truly arrived. That month, *Star Wars Episode II: Attack of the Clones* became the first high-profile, high-budget movie released that was shot on 24-frame-per-second high-definition digital video, using a Sony HDW-F900 camera. However, the lesser-known 2001 movie *Vidocq*, shot with the same camera, may actually hold the honor of being the first movie shot digitally at a quality high enough to approach that of film. Later successes with digital video format came with Michael Mann's *Collateral*, the Oscar-nominated movie starring Tom Cruise and Jamie Foxx. It was shot and edited entirely with digital video–based equipment.

Over the last five years, many internationally renowned filmmakers have embraced the all-digital format, including such notables as Lars von Trier (*Breaking the Waves, Dancer in the Dark, Dogville*), David Fincher (*Fight Club, Panic Room*), Mike Figgis

DIGITAL MOVIEMAKING

Director James Cameron prepares to shoot on the set of *Titanic* in 1997. He predicted that digital moviemaking and projection will revolutionize the cinematic experience for moviegoers worldwide.

(*Leaving Las Vegas*), David Lynch (*Blue Velvet*, the *Twin Peaks* movie and television series, *Mulholland Drive*), and James Cameron (*Titanic*). Some directors, like Robert Rodriguez—who rose to prominence by shooting his first feature film, *El Mariachi*, for only $7,000—believe that "once you go digital, you can never go back." He proves his point with each successive movie he makes by doing everything in his studio in Austin, Texas—from shooting on digital film, editing with digital software, and mixing digital sounds and effects.

One of the biggest reasons digital moviemaking proves attractive for major directors is cost. Today, cameras from companies like Sony, Panasonic, JVC, and Canon offer a variety of choices for shooting high-definition video with less than $10,000 worth of camera equipment. At the high end of the market, there has been an emergence of cameras specifically for digital cinema. These cameras offer a resolution and dynamic range that exceed those of traditional video cameras, which are designed for the limited resolution and dynamic range of broadcast television.

You don't have to be famous to go digital. Thanks to the budget end of the market, there is a greater availability of affordable equipment. This means that anyone can make a digital movie, and more people are doing exactly that.

The Basics of Digital Moviemaking

For nearly a century, the only way to make a movie was with film stock. There are countless stories of youngsters—such as the young Steven Spielberg—being given a Super 8mm camera as a present and beginning to shoot home movies around their neighborhoods, hoping to leverage their work into more lucrative gigs. The new generation has embraced developing technologies, and the most important one is the switch from analog to digital moviemaking. There are two systems that have developed as a result: digital film and digital video.

Digital Film

Digital film refers to moviemaking and performance systems that use a digital representation of the brightness and color of each pixel of the image. As a result, editing the film is easier and more flexible compared to more traditional, analog-based systems. Digital film systems have much higher resolution than digital video systems, both in the spatial dimension (number of pixels) and the tonal dimension (representation of brightness).

Digital Video

Digital video refers to a type of video recording system that uses a digital, rather than analog, representation of the video signal. First introduced in 1983 in a format that was used only by television networks, digital video became popular once the cost and processing could be adapted for the average consumer. Streaming digital video was first introduced in the early 1990s by Apple and its QuickTime software, expanding the applications for digital video considerably over the last decade and a half. Digital video is now used in modern mobile phones, video conferencing systems, and the online distribution of media (through traditional streaming video or via peer-to-peer distribution networks such as Kazaa).

Data Storage

The most vital component of digital movies is how they look. Cinematography, or digital capture, determines this. The film recording process may occur on tape, flash memory drives, hard disks, or other media that can record digital data. As the technology has improved, digital filming has gained mainstream acceptance. Several recent Hollywood movies have been shot digitally, and many equipment vendors have brought digital film products to market, including traditional film camera vendors like Arri and Panavision, and companies that

QuickTime is a multimedia framework developed by Apple, Inc., that can play various kinds of media formats, including digital video, audio, text, animation, and music.

have traditionally focused on consumer and broadcast video equipment, like Sony and Panasonic.

There are two ways to store data while making a digital movie: one is videotape-based, while the other is tapeless. Many people, particularly those coming from a background in broadcast television, are most comfortable with videotape-based workflow. Data (in this case, images and sound) is captured on videotape and then inputted into a computer. Once stored in the computer, the footage is edited and then output in its final format, possibly to a film printer for theatrical exhibition or back to videotape for broadcast use. Original videotapes are kept as an archival medium.

The files generated by the nonlinear editing application contain the information necessary to retrieve footage from the proper tapes, should the footage stored on the computer's hard drive be lost.

With tapeless digital image storage, the images—which are nothing more than digital data—are stored in electronic files. In tapeless workflow, images are usually recorded directly to files on hard disk or flash memory–based "digital magazines." At the end of a shooting day (or sometimes even during the day), the files contained on these digital magazines are downloaded, typically to a large RAID connected to an editing system. RAID stands for "redundant array of independent disks," and it describes a system of multiple hard drives that share or replicate data. Once data is copied from the digital magazines, they are erased and returned to the movie set for use in additional shooting. Archiving is accomplished by backing up the digital files from the RAID to a data tape.

CHAPTER TWO

THE CURRENT STATE OF DIGITAL MOVIEMAKING

Digital filmmaking's popularity initially came about because a slew of directors wanted to try out new technologies for their own work. Resistance set in because producers and movie theater operators claimed they would have to spend a phenomenal amount of money converting each screen for full digital capability. However, current technological advances are pushing resistance aside. These new developments are changing the digital moviemaking landscape in dramatic ways.

The Rise of YouTube

Digital moviemaking wouldn't be getting nearly as much attention if it weren't for the bright idea concocted by

A moviemaker sits at his digital editing console.

YouTube founders Chad Hurley (*left*) and Steve Chen stand on the red carpet outside *GQ* magazine's gala dinner celebrating its eleventh annual *Men of the Year* issue.

Chad Hurley, Jawed Karim, and Steve Chen. In February 2005, after a brainstorming session in Hurley's garage, YouTube, a video-sharing Web site, was born. Three months later the site, with its slogan "Broadcast Yourself," went live, allowing anyone in the world to share their videos. Although there are other video-sharing sites, such as DailyMotion and Revver, none of them have enjoyed the popularity that YouTube has.

There are several reasons for this. First, the site's catchy name is easy to remember. Second, many copyrighted videos, such as the popular *Saturday Night Live* sketch "Lazy Sunday," were uploaded to the site by users without the copyright holders' permission. The resulting

YouTube (YouTube.com) is a wildly popular site that lets users upload, view, and share videos. It was founded in 2005 by Jawed Karim, Chad Hurley, and Steve Chen and features film and TV clips, home videos, music, and more.

"viral" viewing of the videos, fueled by word of mouth, chat rooms, and e-mail, led television networks and other copyright holders to demand the videos' removal. This only increased YouTube's profile and name recognition within the general population.

The most important reason for the site's popularity has to do with the technical coding that makes it easy for users to share their videos. On YouTube, users may submit videos in several common-file formats (such as .mpeg and .avi). YouTube automatically converts them to Flash Video (with extension .flv) and makes them available for online viewing. Flash Video is a popular video format among large hosting sites due to its wide compatibility.

It's what happens outside of YouTube, however, that has really caused the site's popularity to grow. That's because once uploaded, each video is accompanied by the full HTML markup for linking to it and/or embedding it within another page. A small addition to the markup for the latter will make the video autoplay when the page is accessed. With code in hand, a user can then display his or her video directly on the site or blog of choice, and the video can be played directly within the post, not just at the YouTube page. However, autoplaying embedded YouTube videos has been reported to slow down page-loading time or even to cause browsers to crash.

YouTube Celebrities

One of the side effects of YouTube's success is that many amateur digital moviemakers have become celebrities. The first example of a "YouTube celebrity" was Brooke Brodack, a twenty-year-old aspiring actress who uploaded videos of herself using the username "Brookers." She began posting her videos online in September 2005. By June 2006, she had secured a development deal with Carson Daly's production company, making her the first performer discovered on YouTube to be offered a contract from the mainstream media. Since August 2006, she has played a large role on ItsYourShowTv.com, a new Carson Daly–hosted video Web site sponsored by NBC, and she has regularly posted videos there.

A more heartwarming example of a YouTube celebrity is that of Peter, a seventy-nine-year-old English widower and pensioner (retiree) who began uploading videos in which he related anecdotes about his life, military history, and love of motorcycles. His introductory video has been viewed more than two million times and has received warm and enthusiastic comments, such as "I wish you were my grandfather" and "Your stories are interesting and enriching. Keep at it!" This first video was followed by more than a dozen others and made Peter into an Internet celebrity almost overnight. He even received mention in various traditional broadcast news media outlets, such as BBC News (the British Broadcasting Corporation's news network) and GMTV (a British morning news program). As of September 2006, Peter had 20,000 subscribers to his videocasts (the most popular subscription that month and the second-most popular of all time on YouTube).

The most infamous YouTube celebrity turned out to be a hoax. Beginning in June 2006, a fifteen-year-old girl named Bree, using the moniker "Lonelygirl15," began to upload videos shot in her bedroom where she talked about her life, her strict religious upbringing and home schooling, and her best friend Daniel, who liked her "more than a friend." She also made vague references to the occult and obscure religious rituals she was preparing to take part in.

The subtle sense of menace and the continuing storyline—not to mention the girl's good looks and charming geek-girl personality—attracted tens of thousands of fans and much media coverage speculating about whether she was real or fake. In late September 2006, a combination of amateur and journalistic sleuthing brought out the truth: Lonelygirl15 was really Australian

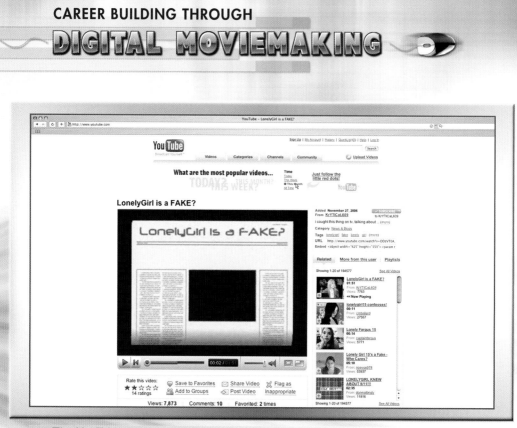

This YouTube page contains a video exploring the Lonelygirl15 phenomenon and its exposure as a fictional story, rather than a truly autobiographical video blog as was first believed.

actress Jessica Rose, and the videos were a product of Ramesh Flinders, a screenwriter and filmmaker from Marin County, California, and Miles Beckett, a surgical residency dropout turned filmmaker.

Despite the revelation that Lonelygirl15 is a fictional character, the videos live on. As of December 2006, ninety-five episodes have aired on YouTube and Revver (another video-sharing site that attaches advertising to user-submitted video clips and shares all ad revenue 50/50 with the creators). More recent installments have continued the adventures of Bree and Daniel as their lives take increasingly melodramatic, thriller-like twists and turns.

Videoblogging

Though Lonelygirl15 turned out to be a manufactured character, her popularity is indicative of the growth not only of YouTube, but also of a certain form of digital moviemaking: the video blog, or vlog. Vlogs often take advantage of Web syndication to allow for the distribution of video over the Internet using either the RSS or Atom syndication formats for automatic aggregation and playback on personal computers and mobile devices (like cell phones and video iPods). Though many vlogs are collaborative efforts, the majority of vlogs and vlog entries are authored by individuals.

Vlogs have been around since 2002, but they did not rise to prominence until 2005. That's when the Yahoo! Videoblogging Group, once considered the center of the vlogging community, saw its membership increase dramatically. That same year, the first Vloggercon, a conference for existing and aspiring videobloggers, took place in New York City. The growth in the popularity of vlogs can be attributed to several factors, such as the release of a new generation of iPods capable of playing video files and the introduction of video into the iTunes Store. The popularity of all types of Internet-based video—such as YouTube—also grew significantly during this same period.

As with many burgeoning Internet trends, vlogging did not become fully mainstream until a major rift took place. One of the most popular videoblogs proved to be *Rocketboom*, a daily three-minute vlog in the vein of Comedy Central's *The Daily Show*, hosted by Jon Stewart. *Rocketboom* was created by Andrew Baron and Amanda

Congdon. It launched in October 2004 with Congdon, a twenty-something blonde who combined good looks and excellent comedic timing, as its host. Her hosting, as well as the show's emphasis on current events and bizarre news stories, attracted a cult following that increased to 70,000 viewers per day after ten months of circulation. By the spring of 2006, 300,000 people were viewing the show regularly. Congdon's success was noted by many media outlets, including *Business Week*, which declared *Rocketboom* "the most popular site of its kind on the Net."

Then, on July 5, 2006, Congdon released a video on her own blog saying she had been "un-boomed" and forced out as host of *Rocketboom*. The *Rocketboom* Web site followed immediately with its version of the story, claiming that she quit in order to prepare for a move to Los Angeles. A media firestorm ensued, resulting in job offers for Congdon—the first bona fide star of the vlog medium—and a greater awareness of videoblogging as a whole.

While Congdon eventually found success with her own production company, as well as a new position with the ABC television network developing video podcasts and producing Web-centric correspondence, *Rocketboom* moved on with a new host, former MTV VJ Joanne Colan. Her hosting was initially greeted with skepticism among those still loyal to Congdon, but Colan soon found an appreciative audience for her mix of humor, substantial interviews, and in-depth field reports.

Congdon may be the most high-profile videoblogger, but several other vloggers have achieved some level of

Darryl Hannah appears in a still from the 1984 film *Splash*. More recently she has become a videoblogger. She focuses on environmentalism and strategies for leading an eco-friendly lifestyle.

success, if not notoriety. On the celebrity front, Daryl Hannah, whose movie appearances include *Splash* and *Kill Bill*, relaunched her Web site as a videoblog in April 2006. In it, she chronicles her life, discusses her celebrity friends, and promotes the environmental causes in which she is active. There has been some criticism that she hopped on the vlog bandwagon, but Hannah's site has nevertheless proven extremely popular.

In November 2006, the annual "Vloggies" for best video blogs in more than thirty categories were awarded. *Ze Frank*, a daily comedy show from the creative mind of longtime Net creator Hosea Frank, won for Best Male Videoblog. The female winner was Ryanne Hodson, an

early adapter to videoblogging (she began in November 2004) who now runs a tutorial site on Freevlog.com. The best comedy vlog award went to *Ask a Ninja*, a cult favorite in which the host—dressed in full Ninja garb— fields viewer questions. (Sample: Q: What is the ideal gift for a ninja? A: Giving a ninja something black is like giving crazy to Angelina Jolie . . . We already have plenty.) The overall winner for Best Video blog was *Alive in Baghdad*, a weekly vlog that, according to its Web site, "brings testimonies from individual Iraqis, footage of daily life in Iraq, and short news segments from Iraq through the work of a team of Americans and Iraqi corre- spondents on the ground." News of the award was greeted with a standing ovation and tremendous enthusiasm.

Machinima

Machinima is defined as filmmaking within a real-time, 3-D virtual environment, often using 3-D videogame technologies. In essence, people will record in-game animation and edit it together with voice recordings to make a film. Though this form of digital moviemaking has been slower to catch on and is seen as less hip and glamorous than its videoblogging cousin, machinima is well on its way to more mainstream success. Machinima can be script-driven, meaning the cameras, characters, and effects are scripted for playback in real time. While similar to animation, the scripting is driven by events and not keyframes. It can also be recorded in real time within the virtual environment, much like filmmaking. The majority of game-specific machinima pieces are produced in this way. Live-produced machinima can thus be created in fashion similar to that of live-action film: the camera records performances, dialogue, and action as they take place.

By combining the techniques of filmmaking, animation production, and the technology of real-time 3-D game engines, machinima makes for a very cost- and time-efficient way to produce films, while preserving a large amount of creative control. This is possible, according to Machinima.org (a repository of information on the subject), because machinima can be shot live or scripted in real time. So it becomes much faster to produce than traditional animation via computer generated images (CGI). CGI is the dominant form of animation and effects seen in live-action movies today. With machinima, multiple takes can be made in real time to get it just right. Or only a few takes can be shot, and if they are flawed, they can simply be adjusted in post-production. CGI doesn't offer this kind of ease, speed, or flexibility.

Additionally, instead of rendering frames of animation or video streams, some machinima is recorded at the data level, only capturing positions, orientation, and other pertinent pieces of information for the 3-D assets to be drawn and animated during playback. Data-recorded machinima allows for editing at the data level, where you can add characters, adjust camera angles, create camera moves, and fine-tune animation. It's much like doing a re-shoot without having to call back the cast and crew, further blurring the lines between production and post-production.

Machinima does have its disadvantages. What can be done in a movie is limited by the genre of the videogame

and the flexibility of the game engine itself. Also, because game engines were primarily designed for game playing and not for making movies, the moviemaking capabilities of game engines—and, consequently, the quality of the produced movies—tend to be limited when compared to 3-D animation software used by professionals.

The earliest roots of machinima can be found in the demoscene, a computer subculture that became established in the 1980s. The demoscene demos are non-interactive software programs containing graphics, music, and visual effects animated in real time. The technological basis for demos is similar to computer and video games. Early demos could even use elements, such as music and sprites (two-dimensional images or animation integrated into a larger scene), which were directly copied from videogames. Unlike machinima, however, demos are nearly always stand-alone programs that are created from scratch. They don't piggyback on a videogame or game engine like machinima does.

In 1992, the game *Stunt Island* was released. It offers users a filmmaking experience by allowing them to position props and cameras, orchestrate stunts, and splice together takes. This was a rudimentary example of machinima, though things did not really pick up until the late 1990s, when filmmakers experimented with videogame platforms created by the games *Doom*, *Quake*, *The Sims*, and *MechWarrior2*, which was the first game to include a limited recording feature with a controllable camera system, allowing for machinima experimentation. Machinima movies have been developed from complex role-playing games such as *World of Warcraft*, *Halo*, *Rome: Total War*, and *Quake*.

Halo 2 is a first-person shooter game with a science-fiction storyline designed for play on Microsoft's Xbox game console. It was released in 2004 as a sequel to the popular *Halo: Combat Evolved*, both developed by Bungie Studios.

On November 4 and 5, 2006, the Academy of Machinima Arts and Sciences held its annual Machinima Festival at the Museum of the Moving Image in Astoria, Queens, in New York City. Founded in 2002, "the event has grown from its humble beginnings as an unofficial adjunct to the 2002 QuakeCon in Mesquite, Texas, to the definitive machinima event held in New York City," according to the festival's mission statement. Aside from screening dozens of new machinima films, the festival awarded its annual Mackie Awards for the best in the field. Best film went to *The Adventures of Bill & John: Danger Attacks at Dawn*. Other categories garnering honors included Best Direction, Best Virtual Performance for Puppeteering

or Virtual Animation, Best Voice Acting, and Best Visual Design, making it quite a different awards show from the Academy of Motion Picture Arts and Sciences annual Academy Awards presentation.

CHAPTER THREE

MAKING A DIGITAL MOVIE

Moviemaking has never been easier or cheaper than it is today. All you need is a good idea, a relatively inexpensive camcorder, and computer equipment to edit and then upload your movie to a Web site or social networking area. No wonder young people are flocking to the field. If you've decided that moviemaking is your dream, it's important to identify what you want to accomplish, set ambitious but realistic goals, and acquire the tools of the trade that you will need to meet those goals.

QUICK TIP

First and foremost is coming up with a creative idea for a movie project. There

---

An amateur moviemaker uses a handheld camcorder to record digital images.

are all sorts of large and small projects ideally suited to digital filmmaking. A simple project is to turn the camera on yourself while reciting a dramatic monologue, acting out a scripted or improvised scene, or performing in a way that's designed to be funny or moving. Whatever the idea is, it's good to plan it out in advance, usually by storyboarding. This means that for each scene you should plan the following:

- The approximate duration/length of the scene
- Location
- Characters
- Dialogue
- Props
- Voice-over narration

Sometimes a full screenplay is necessary. Other times, you can use a rough plan that is partly scripted or provides general guidelines and structure, but allows for some improvisation. If you're really daring, you can try to wing it completely. But the more solid and detailed the plan, the more likely that the movie will be polished and require fewer takes and editing.

The next important consideration is the equipment. There are many varieties of cameras, and this guide is not meant to serve as a consumer report for which is the best camera to get. But in general, aspiring moviemakers will need the following devices: a digital camcorder, a charged battery, a power supply, and a memory card to capture and store the video being shot. Many new digital cameras also have intricate lens capability to zoom in close or pull back for wider shots. They often come with memory cards such as an SD card or Memory Stick/

Memory Stick Pro. This option allows for quick and easy transfer of the digital video from the camera to the PC via a USB connection or through a card reader.

What to Look for in a Digital Camera

- **Check out the LCD screen in daylight, if possible.** Some screens will wash out in bright sunlight, and you'll want to make sure you can easily see what you're recording under any conditions. If you can't see the screen in bright daylight, look for a viewfinder. It can help get the job done without eating up a lot of battery power.

- **Look at the lens's optical zoom ratio instead of the digital zoom ratio.** With a digital zoom, the camcorder is only enlarging the lens's image, instead of really giving you a closer look. The optical zoom spec is more important. You'll want at least a 10X optical zoom.

- **For longer recording times, buy a higher-capacity battery.** The battery that comes with most camcorders only lasts an hour or so. For around $100, you can buy a longer-lasting battery, so factor that into your cost if you think you'll need it. Remember, larger batteries add to the camera's weight.

- **Front-mounted microphones get better results.** Top-mounted microphones tend to capture the voice of the person using the camera and drown out everything else.

- **Buy an external microphone for the best sound.** Factor in an extra $100 to $150 for an external

In 2005, Toshiba unveiled its hard-disk camcorder, the Gigashot V10 (*right*), and its hard-disk audio player, the Gigabeat X30 (*left*). The Gigashot is a hybrid camcorder/digital camera that records high-def video and takes high-res photos.

microphone if you want the best sound possible. Of course, make sure your camcorder has a place for you to plug it in.

- **Try out the camera's controls before you buy.** Sometimes the smallest camcorders can be difficult to use, especially if you have large hands. A larger model may work better for you if it's more comfortable to use.

- **Low-light options let you shoot in the dark.** Many cameras offer an infrared light or long shutter mode to help you capture images in dark settings.

- **Know your format.** Most camcorders use MiniDV, but other formats are available, such as Digital 8 and

MicroMV. Keep in mind that MiniDV is the most widely available—a boon if you find yourself short on tape while on holiday. [Source: *PC World Australia's Digital Video Camera Buying Guide*, April 2005.]

Storage Formats

Once the movie is finished and ready to be uploaded for editing, there are many types of formats to choose from. There are some issues to consider. Do you want to stream the video, or send it in as a complete file? Will your audience be a targeted group, such as an e-mail list, or just one individual? Will it be available to everyone on your homepage? Based on the answers to these questions, you can choose the storage format that best suits your needs.

A popular way to create small audio and video files is to use MPEG, an acronym for Moving Pictures Expert Group—the name of a family of standards used for coding audio-visual information (e.g., movies, video, music) in a digital compressed format. There are several MPEG versions available. MPEG-1 was the earliest format and is still a popular one. It is a good option for Internet distribution of your film over a broadband connection. This is due to the transfer rate of 1500Kbps (bits per second), which is comparable to a high-speed broadband connection. But the most preferred format today is MPEG-4 because it can deliver good video quality at extremely low data rates, even down to 10Kbps. Yet, when needed, the bit rate can be lifted to around 1Mbps, providing near-DVD quality video. DivX, one of the most used formats on the Web for distributing movie titles, is based on the MPEG-4 format.

For more sophisticated videos, MPEG-2 is the format used in DVD video distribution; it has playback rates from around 500 to 1000Kbps. By altering the playback or delivery rate, users can tailor the delivery of a video to meet the speed of a connection, or to store more video on a DVD disc. The arrival of MPEG-2 camcorders allows users to distribute video immediately via the Web through the PC or through wireless technologies such as Bluetooth.

Video Editing

Now that the video is uploaded, it's time to get it ready for editing. Most DV camcorders come with a basic selection of video editing tools, although these applications are generally light versions with some features and tools removed. As you become more experienced, you may want to look at the more powerful options available.

TECH TOOLS For beginners, several software programs, from Windows Movie Maker, Pinnacle Studio 9, and VideoStudio9, provide a mix of guidance and user control to help you create a video that is ready to be viewed almost right away. For those with more experience, it may be better to try more high-end video editing applications. The most popular program in use today is Adobe Premiere (primarily for PC users, but with Mac capabilities as well). Premiere's popularity stems from the variety of its features, including strong color-correction options and new motion controls. On the audio side, AC-3 export, 5.1 surround sound mixing, the ability to record voice recordings to the timeline, and sub frame audio editing provide extra incentives for

Adobe Production Studio is a package of programs that allows users to acquire, edit, enhance, and distribute digital video and audio. It was released in 2006 by Adobe Systems, which developed Photoshop software.

semiprofessionals to use this program. Other products on the high-end side include MediaStudioPro 7 and Pinnacle Edition 5.

Making a Video Blog

For those who are more interested in self-expression than a complete, polished movie product, all that's needed is a camera, a computer, and a broadband Internet connection. The first step is making your video blog and downloading it onto your computer. Each video blog probably shouldn't run longer than a few minutes, since Internet users often have very short attention spans and many other sites competing for their attention.

The Academy of Machinima Arts and Sciences (www.machinima.org) is a non-profit organization that promotes, organizes, and recognizes the growth of machinima filmmaking and filmmakers.

Next, you need to upload your video onto the Internet. You can pay for storage from a hosting company, although some blog sites offer it for free. The process is very simple—akin to attaching a file to an e-mail—so you don't need an enormous amount of technical expertise. Posting your video—and a still image to alert surfers to its content—to your blog is the final piece of the puzzle. Some HTML is required, but step-by-step instructions are provided on the blog site of your choice. Voila! A video blog is born.

Making Machinima

At the present time, there are two different methods for creating a digital movie out of a video game, as

Machinima.org's Frequently Asked Questions explain. The first involves recording the output of your favorite game to video. This approach has you record the output of the game to a video source (camcorder or VCR) and then capture this footage back into your computer for editing and post-production. The other path is bit more ambitious, as it involves using an underlying 3-D game engine but creating entirely new characters and sets. Once these new elements are created, the production process is very similar to that of the first method described—recording the engine output, capturing the footage into a computer, and editing it with editing software.

CHAPTER FOUR

CAREER OBJECTIVES AND ETHICAL CONCERNS

At a time when the average computer user is voted *Time* magazine's 2006 Person of the Year, and when much of that honor is due to the viral spread of digital videos throughout the Internet and all around the world, important issues must be addressed. The process and act of moviemaking can give rise to surprisingly thorny questions. These include:

- Why make a digital film?
- Who is the intended audience?
- What are the filmmaker's ethical responsibilities?
- What are the consequences of digital movie-making fame?

Acetate-based film technology is rapidly being replaced by digital recording, projection, and storage.

Why Make a Digital Film?

There are many reasons for teens to make their own digital films. These can range from keeping a digital journal or video blog, to expressing personal beliefs and ideology, to just having fun telling a story or crafting skits. Some experiment with digital movies as a way to learn the craft of filmmaking and cinematic storytelling. Because going digital is cheaper and quicker than using film stock, storytelling can become much easier.

Because of YouTube's incredible popularity, many teens will want to "cash in" and make movies as a way of marketing themselves or making money. As explained in chapter 2, several "YouTube celebrities" have emerged in an organic, viral marketing fashion, while the success of others (such as Lonelygirl15) proved to be a more calculated, complex endeavor. Keep in mind, however, that "going viral" is a relatively rare occurrence, and Web-based fame is rarer still and short-lived.

Who Is the Intended Audience?

Depending on whether your moviemaking goal is entertainment, enlightenment, social awareness, or some other objective, your target audience will change. A film that is meant to be funny will probably appeal more to younger viewers, but the type of humor may also resonate with an older audience, too. Many YouTubers and videobloggers have a particular niche in mind, and finding out what that is will be a critical undertaking.

What Are the Filmmaker's Ethical Responsibilities?

This question should be answered on several fronts. First, there is a general concern about using digital equipment of any sort, not just cameras, because of the opportunity that exists with digital technology to manipulate the images with software such as Photoshop and other tools of the trade.

An excellent example of how digital manipulation can distort truth is a recent short film made by the cosmetic company Dove. In it, a model of moderate attractiveness sits in a makeup chair as makeup is lavishly layered on her face. Afterward, Photoshop retouching alters the contours of her face, extends her hair, changes her eye color, color-balances her skin, and makes her look like a completely different person. The results are astonishing, but not surprising, as many fashion magazines use this same process to refine the look of the models gracing their covers and inside pages.

Another concern has more to do with content distortion. Even if you want your film to make a pointed editorial statement that is not journalistically objective, you must still take care to treat the subject matter carefully and present information factually and fairly. Don't ignore or leave out information that undercuts or challenges your argument. You should adjust your argument to accommodate the facts. If your film is supposed to be objective, then it is of crucial importance to get the facts as accurate as possible and to represent your views in a professional, even-handed manner.

Film stills from the *Lord of the Rings* trilogy appear above, demonstrating how computer-generated images are created by the layering of digital animation.

A third concern has to do with originality. Is the content of the film—its images, soundtrack, dialogue, etc.—yours, or did you take it from somewhere else? A key problem with YouTube is that many digital filmmakers do not ask for permission before uploading other people's films and incorporating some of their images. This uploaded material may be content copyrighted, meaning that its use by someone else requires permission and perhaps a fee.

Though copyright issues are generally beyond the scope of this book, this is an issue that will become increasingly important as file-sharing becomes more common and moviemakers and studios attempt to protect their content and prevent illegal use of it. One way of preventing misuse of content is with a Creative Commons license. This allows other Web sites to link and share your files as long as they acknowledge who it belongs to and where it came from.

What Are the Consequences of Digital Moviemaking Fame?

One consequence of the sudden celebrity that can come with a digital video that "goes viral" has to do with the increasing efforts of "citizen journalism" by amateur filmmakers who chronicle the world and share it with a wide audience. People who capture crimes being committed or incidents of police brutality may be serving the cause of truth and justice, but they may also become targets of revenge. In other instances, a moviemaker may film someone who doesn't realize he or she is being filmed or who hasn't given his or her permission

YouTube – George Jefferies

George Jefferies

Rate this video:
★★★★☆
7 ratings

Save to Favorites   Share Video   Flag as
Add to Groups   Post Video   Inappropriate

Views: **4,604**   Comments: **4**   Favorited: **2 times**

Honors: 3   Links: 0

Citizen journalism is not a new phenomenon. A home movie filmed by George Jeffries about ninety seconds before the assassination of John F. Kennedy was made public and posted on sharing sites like YouTube.com in February 2007.

for the images to be broadcast publicly. Depending on the activities filmed, that person's reputation may suffer, or he or she may become subject to job termination, public taunts, humiliation, or even attacks. That person, in turn, may sue the filmmaker for damages.

One unforeseen consequence of YouTube videos bears some similarity to what happens with blogging. One blogger, Heather Armstrong, wrote unflattering commentaries about her employer on her popular blog and was fired as a result—the first blogger to suffer that fate. In some instances, employees have gotten into trouble not for speaking badly of their employers but for misusing company time and property. Terence

Tan, a temporary employee with the Singapore manpower agency Starhub, was fired by the company for making and distributing a video depicting Tan and other employees wearing Starhub uniforms and "horsing around" on the company premises. Though the company was not named in the initial news articles, Starhub's human resources director, Chan Hoi San, wrote a letter in defense of its actions and denied that active dismissal took place. San claimed that Tan was merely no longer needed at Starhub and was therefore returned to his temp agency.

Citizen Journalism

One of the unexpected side effects of the digital moviemaking and YouTube boom is the rise in citizen journalism. All it takes is a cameraphone and a broadband connection to make raw, unedited footage available on the Internet and shine a light into dark corners of the United States and the world, whether on a personal or a political level.

One avenue that has changed dramatically as a result of citizen journalism is the political campaign. Instead of politicians trying to attract attention and solicit votes with campaign ads, now the Web is turning things around to focus attention back on the politicians. This new dynamic was clearly illustrated in the case of S. R. Sidarth, a University of Virginia college student working for the campaign of Democrat Senate hopeful James Webb. Part of his job was to track incumbent and Republican opponent George Allen at his campaign stops.

On August 11, 2006, Allen singled Sidarth out in the crowd with a long, rambling riff. "This fellow here, over

Video of the 2005 tsunami in Southeast Asia appears on YouTube. Thousands of examples of citizen journalism—events captured by people with camcorders and cameraphones—are on this and other sites.

here with the yellow shirt, Macaca or whatever his name is, he's with my opponent," Allen said. And later: "So welcome, let's give a welcome to Macaca here! Welcome to America and the real world of Virginia!" A Macaca is a type of monkey, and many people took the comments directed at Sidarth, an American of Indian descent, to be racist. The video clip was uploaded to YouTube and, to date, has been viewed more than 500,000 times.

Perhaps as a result of the viral spread of the video clip (along with other information that came to light regarding other instances of Senator Allen's racial insensitivity), Allen's popularity waned, and he lost his re-election bid to Webb in a tight contest. That the clip broadcasted far and wide an embarrassing incident on

the campaign trail that may otherwise have gone unreported may have swung voters away from Allen and toward Webb.

Other examples of citizen journalism have focused on civil rights and police brutality. A search on YouTube for the terms "police brutality" found almost 800 videos, including ones that claim to show police violence in the United States and as far away as Egypt and Hungary. In the fall of 2006, no less than three separate incidents of brutality in California alone found their way to YouTube, thanks to cameraphone recordings by bystanders.

One of them, showing two Los Angeles Police Department officers beating twenty-four-year-old William Cardenas while arresting him on charges of receiving stolen property, caught the attention of the FBI, which has now launched a probe into the matter. A second incident, which took place at a library of the University of California–Los Angeles, shows a student in the process of leaving the premises being stunned by a taser gun fired at him by campus police.

As the mainstream media focus more on such incidents, some law enforcement agencies have installed cameras in squad cars to protect officers against false allegations. This may also serve the purpose of encouraging them to use restraint when arresting suspects.

Other law enforcement agencies, however, have used YouTube for their own benefit. In December 2006, police in Hamilton, Ontario, Canada, used it to help solve the November murder of twenty-two-year-old Ryan Milner in a parking lot after a rock concert. This was the first time Hamilton police have utilized a video Web posting in an

A video clip depicting an act of alleged police brutality appears on YouTube. The site contains many clips relating to police actions, crimes captured on camera, car accidents, and the aftermath of natural disasters.

investigation, and to the best of its knowledge, the first time that law enforcement has ever used it as a direct investigative tool, according to Staff Sergeant Jorge Lasso. The one-minute, twelve-second clip showed footage from a surveillance video of a man wearing a baseball cap with the word JOKER on the front. After the clip was viewed more than 30,000 times, twenty-four-year-old George Gallow turned himself in to police and was ultimately charged with second-degree murder. This case may represents things to come as more police departments use YouTube and video-sharing as investigative tools. Surveillance and home/cell phone video offer excellent proof of what actually happened and who is guilty of what.

As a result of the growth of citizen journalism, companies are trying to find a way to make money on it and to increase the visibility of the medium. Yahoo! recently launched You Witness News, a portal where would-be citizen journalists can upload their videos. The site has been slow to catch on, as YouTube still dominates this particular market. There is also a greater concern among filmmakers regarding You Witness News over how much of the money will end up in their pockets (as opposed to Yahoo!'s).

One consequence of the proliferation of amateur videos is that viewers can become desensitized to the violence or depravity that is often caught on camera. "The first reaction by people is one of outrage," said Eugene O'Donnell, a professor of police studies at the John Jay College of Criminal Justice in New York City, in a news story by MSNBC.com. "But the more you see police officers using force on tape, the more you get used to it."

Protecting Intellectual Copyright

The violation of a copyright on original material is a serious problem faced by the major corporations that own movie and television studios, as their products are often illegally distributed via video-sharing programs without anyone paying money to see them. But these kinds of copyright violations don't just affect big companies; they can be an issue for anyone making a digital movie. So how would one go about protecting his or her work?

This issue faced Fritz Grobe and Stephen Voltz, the masterminds behind the enormously popular video

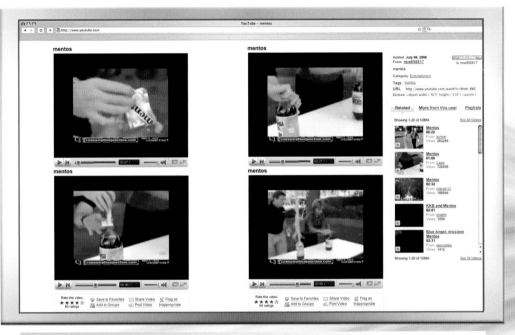

A video clip of the infamous Mentos and Diet Coke experiment appears on YouTube. Its creators, Fritz Grobe and Stephen Voltz, received no proceeds from YouTube for the video, despite the fact that millions have viewed it there.

showing the explosive results when Mentos breath mints are dropped into bottles of Diet Coke. As they told *Business Week* in 2006, they had made $25,000 through an advertising-sharing deal with Revver, but most of the 4.1 million page views of the video (as of June 2006) came through Google Video and YouTube, which did not have any ad-sharing deals in place. Thus, Grobe and Voltz lost out on hundreds of thousands of dollars of revenue. This opened a spirited debate about copyright and whose interests should be favored when considering intellectual property laws—big corporations or tiny upstarts hoping to make a reasonable living from their creative labors.

Answers to these copyright questions are still hard to come by. Revver offers a partial solution. Creative Commons licensing, where copyright is indicated but sharing is allowed, is another partial answer, but questions of intellectual property, fair use, and proper reimbursement may be the single most important issue facing digital filmmakers of any stripe.

CHAPTER FIVE
FINDING SUCCESS IN THE DIGITAL MOVIEMAKING WORLD

There are many avenues to success for those who intend to begin their careers—or just explore their interests—in digital moviemaking. But for every success story, there are thousands of people whose quest for fame and fortune fall by the wayside, just as with any creative pursuit. So how is an aspiring teen digital moviemaker able to get his or her name out there?

Strong Content

Videos and films, whatever the subject matter and the distribution source, live and die by their content. If it's good, funny, provocative, revealing, shocking, and/or

Moviemaking tools old and new include film stock, videotapes, DVDs, digital cameras, and personal computers.

insightful, then there will be an audience, however limited, for the digital movie.

QUICK TIP

A Professional Attitude: Many digital filmmakers work on their own, but a great majority do not. Being able to work with others, meet deadlines; handle actors and crew, looking out for their needs as well as your own; and make content available in an easy and efficient manner are all extremely important qualities for a would-be digital filmmaker.

Viral Marketing

Should the digital movie's content attract an audience, chances are good that the initial viewers will tell other people and word of mouth will kick in accordingly. Though ads, product placement, and marketing campaigns can all help to increase awareness, organic word of mouth is ultimately the best tool at a filmmaker's disposal.

That is how twenty-two-year-old Lasse Gjertsen, a Norwegian digital filmmaker, became one of YouTube's instant sensations. His three-minute video, "Hyperactive," features a hip-hop song whose "instrumentation" is composed wholly of sounds uttered from his mouth. It proved so popular since first uploaded to YouTube in May 2006 that the Cartoon Network used the song in a commercial for one of its morning television shows. But Gjertsen's popularity crested when he released "Amateur," a piano/drum duet featuring stop-motion video in which each musical note corresponded to a single frame of video. According to the *Wall Street Journal*, the resulting video was viewed more than 1.5 million times, and Gjertsen recently went to Italy to direct a music video.

The cult popularity of Lasse Gjertsen's homemade video for his song "Amateur," and its predecessor "Hyperactive," is due largely to its appearance on YouTube, where it "went viral."

With healthy ambition, a video camera, and a broadband connection, the door to video moviemaking success is wide open. You only need to be willing to work hard to step through it.

GLOSSARY

blog Short for Weblog, it is a frequently updated Web site, often in journal format. It can now accommodate audio, video, and other multimedia formats.

Bluetooth A wireless connection that enables devices to exchange information.

brightness Refers to the intensity of the video display; it is defined by the amount of light produced by the display.

broadband High-speed Internet connection.

CGI Stands for computer-generated image, a term used when computers have created an image seen on computer, television, or film screen.

citizen journalism The act of citizens playing an active role in the process of collecting, reporting, analyzing, and disseminating news and information.

digital camera Camera that records pictures electronically, rather than on film.

digital film Cinema production and performance systems that work by using a digital representation of the brightness and color of each pixel of the image.

digital video Video where all of the information representing images has been digitized, allowing it to be more flexible and rapidly manipulated or displayed by a computer.

LCD Stands for liquid crystal display, a low-power monitor often used on the top and/or rear of a digital camera to display settings or the photo itself.

machinima Filmmaking using animation, video games, and other real-time tools.

mixing Used in sound recording, audio editing, and sound systems to balance the relative volume and frequency content of a number of sound sources.

pixel Smallest unit of a digital image.

RAID Acronym for redundant array of independent disks, a data storage scheme in which multiple hard drives share and/or replicate data.

real time Transmission that occurs right away, without any perceptible delay.

surround sound Audio intended to heighten realism by emanating from in front of, behind, and to the side of the viewer.

videoblog A Weblog that uses video as its primary presentation format; often abbreviated to "vlog."

wireless Refers to the type of broadband connection in which information is sent from and arrives at a computer through transmission towers.

YouTube Immensely popular Web site designed for sharing videos.

FOR MORE INFORMATION

Academy of Interactive Arts and Sciences
23622 Calabasas Road, Suite 220
Calabasas, CA 91302
(818) 876-0826
Web site: http://www.interactive.org

Center for Digital Imaging Arts at Boston University
282 Moody Street
Waltham, MA 02453
(781) 209-1700
Web site: http://www.cdiabu.com

Cyber Film School/Northwest Film School
301 W. Holly Street M-5
Bellingham, WA 98225
(360) 738-1616
Web site: http://www.cyberfilmschool.com

Entertainment Software Association
575 7th Street NW, Suite 300
Washington, DC 20004
Web site: http://www.theesa.com

Los Angeles Film School
6363 Sunset Boulevard, Suite 500
Los Angeles, CA 90028
(877) 9LA-FILM (952-3456)
Web site: http://www.lafilm.com/

Museum of the Moving Image
35 Avenue at 36 Street
Astoria, NY 11106
(718) 784-4520
Web site: http://www.movingimage.us/site/site.php

New York Film Academy
100 E. 17th Street
New York, NY 10003
(212) 674-4300
Web site: http://www.nyfa.com/

Tisch School of the Arts at New York University
Cinema Studies
721 Broadway, 6th floor
New York, NY 10003
(212) 998-1600

UCLA School of Theater, Film and Television
102 East Melnitz Hall
Box 951622
Los Angeles, CA 90095-1622
(310) 825-5761
Web site: http://www.tft.ucla.edu/

USC School of Cinematic Arts
Attn: Animation and Digital Arts Program
University Park, LPB 200C
Los Angeles, CA 90089-2211
(213) 740-3986
Web site: http://www-cntv.usc.edu/

Web Sites

Due to the changing nature of Internet links, Rosen Publishing has developed an online list of Web sites related to the subject of this book. This site is updated regularly. Please use this link to access the list:

http://www.rosenlinks.com/dcb/cbdm

FOR FURTHER READING

Aronson, Ian David. *DV Filmmaking: From Start to Finish*. Sebastopol, CA: O'Reilly Media, 2006.

Billups, Scott. *Digital Moviemaking: All the Skills, Techniques and Moxie You'll Need to Turn Your Passion Into a Career*. 2nd ed. Studio City, CA: Michael Wiese Productions, 2003.

Billups, Scott. *Digital Moviemaking: The Filmmaker's Guide to the 21st Century*. Studio City, CA: Michael Wiese Productions, 2000.

Bryant, Stephanie. *Videoblogging for Dummies*. New York, NY: For Dummies, 2006.

Dedman, Jay, and Joshua Paul. *Videoblogging*. Hoboken, NJ: John Wiley & Sons, 2006.

Gross, L., and L. Ward. *Digital Moviemaking*. 5th ed. New York, NY: Wadsworth, 2006.

Hanson, Matt. *The End of Celluloid: Film Futures in the Digital Age*. Hove, England: RotoVision, 2004.

Jenkins, Henry, et al. *Confronting the Challenges of Participatory Culture: Media Education for the 21st Century*. Chicago, IL: The MacArthur Foundation. 2006.

Kenworthy, Chris. *Digital Video Production Cookbook*. Sebastopol, CA: O'Reilly Media, 2005.

Kiryanov, D. *Digital Moviemaking with Pinnacle Studio Plus 10*. Wayne, PA: A-List, 2005.

Lanier, Troy, and Clay Nichols. *Filmmaking for Teens: Pulling Off Your Shorts*. Studio City, CA: Michael Wiese Productions, 2005.

Newton, D., et al. *Digital Filmmaking 101: An Essential Guide to Producing Low-Budget Movies.* Studio City, CA: Michael Wiese Productions, 2001.

Shaner, Pete, and Gerald Everett Jones. *Digital Filmmaking for Teens.* Boston, MA: Course Technology PTR, 2004.

Verdi, Michael, et al. *Secrets of Videoblogging.* Berkeley, CA: Peach Pit, 2006.

BIBLIOGRAPHY

"Buying Guide—Digital Video Cameras." *PC World Australia*. 2005. Retrieved December 10, 2006 (http://www.pcworld.idg.com.au/index.php/id;1847886895;pp;2#dvandtheweb).

Corliss, R. "Can This Man Save the Movies (Again)?" *Time*. March 20, 2006. Retrieved November 30, 2006 (http://www.time.com/time/magazine/article/0,9171,1172229-6,00.html).

Cruz, M. "Digital Movie-Makers Challenge Critic." *Philippines Inquirer*. October 31, 2006. Retrieved November 30, 2006 (http://services.inquirer.net/print/print.php?article_id=29832).

Green, H. "A Different Take on Copyright Battles (YouTube vs. the World)." *Business Week*. June 29, 2006. Retrieved December 23, 2006 (http://www.businessweek.com/the_thread/blogspotting/archives/2006/06/a_different_tak.html?campaign_id=search).

Grossman, L., et al. "Best Invention: YouTube." *Time*. December 2006. Retrieved November 30, 2006 (http://www.time.com/time/2006/techguide/bestinventions/inventions/youtube2.html).

Lee, E. "YouTube's Video Boom a 'Social Phenomenon.'" *The San Francisco Chronicle*. October 10, 2006. Retrieved December 2, 2006 (http://www.sfgate.com/cgibin/article.cgi?f=/c/a/2006/10/10/YOUTUBE.TMP).

Manovich, L. "What Is Digital Cinema?" 2004. Retrieved November 30, 2006 (http://www.manovich.net/TEXT/digital-cinema.html).

Marino, P. "Machinima: Filmmaking's Destiny." O'Reilly Digital Media. September 8, 2004. Retrieved November 30, 2006 (http://digitalmedia.oreilly.com/2004/09/08/machinima.html).

McCrank, J. "YouTube Helps Find Murder Suspect." Reuters. December 21, 2006. Retrieved December 23, 2006 (http://today.reuters.com/news/articlenews.aspx?type = technologyNews&storyID = 2006-12-22T150829Z_01_MOL163098_RTRUKOC_0_US-CRIME-YOUTUBE.xml&WTmodLoc = TechNewsHome_C1_%5BFeed%5D-9).

Poniewozik, J. "The Beast with a Billion Eyes." *Time*. December 16, 2006. Retrieved December 18, 2006 (http://www.time.com/time/magazine/article/0,9171,1570702,00.html).

Prism Business Media. "2nd Annual Pixie Awards Recognize Top Web Movie-Makers." Digital Content Producer. September 25, 2001. Retrieved November 30, 2006 (http://digitalcontentproducer.com/news/video_nd_annual_pixie/).

Roxborough, S., and C. Masters. "Europe Sets Its Sights on Web Video." *The Hollywood Reporter*. December 19, 2006. Retrieved December 20, 2006 (http://www.hollywoodreporter.com/hr/content_display/international/news/e3i2d2333041a2e6510d2476a67dcfdde1c).

Rutkoff, A. "An Unrefined Musician Uses Stop-Motion Video to Play Catchy Tune." *The Wall Street*

Journal. December 12, 2006. Retrieved
December 15, 2006 (http://online.wsj.com/
public/article/SB1165813816808463273-
u6NlXOnRBxZ6qCKc4WoFeWQ_wgo_20071212.html).

Sherwin A. "Is This the Way to Vlogging Stardom?" *The
Times* (London). May 21, 2005. Retrieved
December 10, 2006 (http://technology.timesonline.
co.uk/article/0,,20411-1621172,00.html).

Shuster, F. "The YouTube Generation." *The Long Beach
Press-Telegram.* October 3, 2006. Retrieved
December 2, 2006 (http://www.presstelegram.com/
music/ci_4436751).

Thomas, J. "Digital Video: The Final Frontier." *Library
Journal.* January 15, 2004. Retrieved November 30,
2006 (http://www.libraryjournal.com/article/
CA371213.html&).

"Video Triggers FBI Probe of L.A. Arrest." Associated
Press. November 10, 2006. Retrieved December 2,
2006 (http://www.msnbc.msn.com/id/15649790/).

"What Is Machinima?" Machinima.org. August 2005.
Retrieved November 30, 2006 (http://www.
machinima.org/machinima-faq.html).

INDEX

About the Author

Miriam Segall is a writer based in New York City, where she writes on a variety of topics, including technology journalism, blogging, and other digital, Internet, and computer technology matters.

Photo Credits

Cover and pp. 1, 49 © www.istockphoto.com; p. 4 (right) © Karen Bleier/Getty Images; pp. 6, 30 © Yoshikazu Tsuno/Getty Images; p. 8 © Merie Wallace/Getty Images; p. 13 © www.istockphoto.com/Dennis Sabo; p. 14 © Robyn Beck/Getty Images; p. 21 © Globe Photos Inc; p. 25 © Chris Hondros/Getty Images; p. 27 © www.istockphoto. com/Yiannos Loannou; p. 36 © www.istockphoto.com/ Mika Makkonen; p. 39 © Warner Bros./courtesy Everett Collection.

Designer: Nelson Sá